Like a Thread to Follow

Poems and Sketches

Sam Rasnake

for Mary

Remember every sunrise, every sunset –
and our path between them

in memory of

Maureen Seaton
"My life is a circle in the high grass."

&

Kelly Cherry
"We will go into the unknown together,
drawing the long sentence of ourselves after us"

Works by Sam Rasnake

Necessary Motions

Lessons in Morphology

Tales of Brave Ulysses (Poetry Series)

Religions of the Blood

Inside a Broken Clock

Cinéma Vérité

World within the World

Like a Thread to Follow

Contents

III Streaming: Coming Unhinged – Unhinged Already

Music in the soul can be heard by the universe.
— Lao Tzu

*The piece of music is nothing without
the act of interpretation.*
— Hélène Grimaud

Begin with the Song

the first words hidden along
the irresistible edges of rocks
find their way to the sea then

a bowl of drunken haze leaving
whispers only for the cave with
its promises of greatness but none

can match the woman who has
the world's story in her fingers
has the will to shape it this way

or that each night for as long as
it takes it will take everything
she is unlike the blundering man

who wouldn't know the words
if you tongued them into his ear
all he will remember is the tongue

– after the story of Odysseus and Penelope

I

Vinyl:

Something More to Say

A World Full of Lies

It's not dark yet, but it's gettin' there
– Bob Dylan

No Direction Home

I used to believe in the sky, then it bled steel
over green mountains and burned all rivers to dust.
I used to believe in the mouths of children until
I grew sick of my name on their tongues, so I took pliers
to the one voice, plastered their faces on milk cartons
& websites, buses & billboards so I could sleep.
And I slept.

       I trusted oceans, moon in the water,
and praises lost in the wind's throat, before the world
made good its promise, before the desert coughed up
any might have, should have, wish I had.

       Once,
I believed in silence, but I don't believe
that anymore. The fire's too strong, the tundra
too deep, the masters of war too busy. Your eyes follow
these words, so you think you know what I'm saying.
I once hoped the salt of night would give me direction
but I've learned to stay put, and I do it well.

Lay Down Your Weary Tune

The words are so heavy I can't carry them
The words sit, their mountains of mercy
        and grief, on both shoulders of my tongue

But when I say them,
        a cold river shakes loose the gorge

When I say them – all that impossible truth
tips over the edge, down into the clearest,
the deepest of pools
        where thin walls of fish in tangles
        of light and shade above smoothed stones
        dream me back to a rage of blue

"Stars above the barren trees"

> *– after "Blind Willie McTell," Bob Dylan,*
> The Bootleg Series, vols. 1-3

"When I'm gone, and you're on the winter path
above the river – You know the one I mean –
box in hand, ready to finish the promise –
You'll have your doubts, I know...
And me? I never knew anything,

never laughed, or if I did, my face would go
into shock – A relaxed, steady blank has always
been my way – Never learned enough, never
suffered enough – not nearly so – no slave ship
rubbed my skin raw, no single thread of smoke

above the Badlands, no hidden, cooking still
by an icy creek along the Blue Ridge – no way out –
no woman at her desk, head down, hands empty,
everything a cracked mirror that's not her own...

It's all my curse – I'm left with all the things
I can't unsay, unsee, undo... There are words
you must say – Say it all – Leave nothing out –
then listen"

I'm gazing out the window
of the St. James Hotel
and I know no one can sing the blues
like Blind Willie McTell

The snow finishes its quilting – No one on the roads,
all the houses, dark – A mist of voice dusts the tree line,
the hoot owl watches from her limb, and like an almost
remembered story, the long river finds its sea

Delta, 1948

Roads cross.

Robinsonville.
Stovall.
Clarksdale.
Greenwood.

Smell the rain.
Smell corn whiskey as it cooks.

Houses, fields, signs slide by like old totems.
Telephone poles hang from the sky here.
Arms dangle from rolled-down windows.
Trains, trailing new electric eyes, head north,
but they don't shake the ground like they used to.

Clapboard walls of churches rot.

Galvanized machines will pick this field if the levee holds.
And it will. Business is business. That's the rule.

Listen to the trees at night, to the trucks out on the 82.
Listen for the wind.
If you're still, you can hear the Yazoo drift
all the way to Vicksburg.

Sometimes there's a radio:

Quartet in C Minor, Op. 18, No. 4
Beethoven

Allegro ma non tanto

Translation

P: When I cry, my tears let you know who I am. What I want from you is a dry space to soak up grief. Some of it is mine. Some of it is the world's. The silence lets me know you're there, in what is allowed, in what I carry into my different rooms. I've sized each room for my mood. And the room where I sit, now, alone, in front of a monitor is the only one I know. It is my safe room. My words are safe. And when I'm done here, the room where I will go to sleep is my heart room. It's tiny. I have to let go of so much to get through the door. But when I'm inside, I blow myself up like a fish, then squeeze against plaster, and squeeze so tightly that the walls begin to crack, exposing studs underneath that hold up slices of dark sky.

*

O: I'm not sleeping now. What I am doing is thinking my body to your bed, your sheets, my heat against yours, and, without your even knowing, I listen an hour to your breathing, stealing each caesura, lines I have always known.

I listen to fill your space with my own breathing, couplet against couplet, companion pieces in a narrative, a *ms* lost in the deep shadows of both our skulls.

*

O: —P is making sense. The words she overhears she writes down in a small notebook she carries with her, always. She listens. She writes. Listens. Everything fits. Someone comes up to her on the street. And P says, "true popular music?" or "genealogy of morals?" or, and this one is my favorite, "it's stupid and yet?" Every word a question.

*

P: *After years of sleeping, I realize*
the need for waking, for touching,
for the gift that doesn't need to be
held, for the holding that always
wants more than can possibly be
expected. After years of this,
I should know the story by heart,
now. After years of reading
between your whispers and
my having to speak. [scribbled in a journal]

*

O: I feel delicious and wicked, as though the words I intend
are not the ones you hear but are the words that would fill
the world if the world had been another world.

    *

P: *a poet inside a hamster's wheel, finding the end*

    *

O: What I most believe in is an order. A tree falls
in the Amazon basin and fists of smoke drift
over a slender roof, disappear into the vast
Tibetan cold. You eat Indian take-out.
I read French in translation,
a text on philosophy,
a book of dreams.
"what's buried is about to explode"

       – to the hard land of the winter

Scherzo: Andante scherzoso quasi allegretto

Sonnet with a Missing Line

> *– after a photograph of globe lilies*

The wet blooms of *albus rubellus* hide their secrets,
have little in common with the table where I write
these words, half a world away, in the deep hours.
They were a surprise, fragile questions of rain,
the will and can't of living. I'm sure the photographer
couldn't have guessed my struggles with language or
your need for words, but here's the picture. It carries
truth on a determined back – like the massive steps
leading to a rooftop patio overlooking the sea
in Godard's *Contempt*. These petals loom, like
talismans, their bold and certain heads over
our economies that beg us to "deny, deny,
deny" the slow improbabilities of change.

> *– the sirens sweetly singing*

Menuetto: Allegretto; Trio

What I Should Have Written

Loss is that perfect discovery of what
the tongue and eye believe to be true.
Some things we lose in out of way places
or find where we have no expectations.

Everything we know, everything that is real,
waits in the next room or in cyberspace
which is nowhere and is everywhere,
and that waiting is sweet, bitter, exact.

Sometimes we can't tell the difference
between the here and the need. A poverty
of words is the lost connection, so I breathe,
your lungs contract. You inhale, I whisper.

      – touching the distant sands

Allegro; Prestissimo

Desire Is the Final Word

The insides of volcanoes are addictive,
their hot, liquid stone, smoothing all
your words so that when you speak
a story slips its leg into lovemaking,
your own legs a clamp holding me
to truth, my body, a field at the mercy
of storm, shaking under yours.
What I groan could be a poem
if you would sweat it onto paper,
so that years from now, we both
could climb sheer walls of stanza
to the first line and stare into the maw
of this moment, this late, beautiful hour
that belongs to what we most desire.

– where the sky loves the sea

Decades have fallen away now – and what is noted is how distance begins to shrink itself – disappear against the aches of time, against the will to hold on, against any resistance to what is lasting – how the vision morphs, how words shift and begin saying other things, begin saying other truths that are learned only from the inside. Desire is such a fickle master.

What is vital – we finally recognize – is the world outside the window can never equal the one in which we move, can never replace what we have, and that's the beauty of it all – and the danger. One can never see the same sunrise again. Once it's gone, it's not coming back. There will be other days. Absolutely. But not that day. And music? It has its place, surely, an imperfect performance – but a familiar one. That is what we've come to expect.

Most roads remain untraveled. The paths untouched. Forests grow thick and beautiful. A determined heart must be forgiving. Life has become an endless blurting of slogans. What once was true, remains so. One touch shapes another, then before you know it, your world has imploded, yet there you stand, while everything around you burns, a match flaming closer to your fingers, but you're oblivious to any right or wrong. Stop while you can still breathe. Don't do it. You never did.

The music – even after all hands have stopped moving, all mouths and eyes have shriveled away, and the feet are still – won't end. It will keep.

Note: Do keep in mind that the rating system is arbitrary at best, personal in the deepest sense, and an unexplainable blurring of absolute and relative – so much so that universal lines are neither expected nor are they possible. In fact, let me state for the record that if they were possible, we wouldn't accept them. Think what you will, but the poem and life – for that matter – are worth the commitment to ponder, are worth the notes to gather. Read on. Let the music play.

– Anonymous

Exile on Main St.

– Nellcôte, Villefranche-sur-Mer, 1971

In it *and* not of it is how to begin. With the sweet and bitter
fruit of carrying the whole of loss in your veins, in the scars
of a would-be lifetime out of control, out of bounds, a freak
of time and place, with the eyeball pressed to the crowd,
all anger and rage – all anger and rage. We are not from
here. The desperation of spent flowers on the mantle, of
rolled paper on the table, empty bottles about the floor –
Fellini, with a raw touch of smoke & flesh & food & wine
for the radical heart's darkest hunger. Through a door and
down the stairs, the guitar's hard-edged howl, smearing
over cool stones of a basement wall, with its new vocabulary
of hot and dingy to percussive shots of kick and boom.
The sax is a slow river, all misted over, in the decadent
drift of summer nights – no roads leading anywhere,
no want to find one, no dawn to come scratching at
the window to be let in.

– after Stones in Exile, *a 2010 documentary
by Stephen Kijak*

October 1988

– after Leonard Cohen

Everybody knows the plague is coming, and with that start
you've touched the core. Everybody knows something on
someone, knows something that isn't vital but is the thing
you'll want like rain to moss. What everybody knows is
truth is its own opiate, but the pleasures disappear in a
smokeless room of voices that refuse sleep to give enough
to darkness. Everybody, but everybody, gives an ear when
the voice mellows, when the blood thickens, when the hands
sweat rum onto paper so the softer edges of the body fold
into the poem: "the plague, everybody knows, is coming".
Ice melts in the glass, then shadows fall over the printed
page. I get up from my writing table, turn off the light,
and climb the stairs.

Variations on a Theme by Pina Bausch

Words are of no help. I know exactly
what I'm looking for, but not with the head.
It's in the body already. Every detail,

every move finds something new – the dirt
of spring, a full moon on water, silence.
Threads of sadness in the hands, in the touch,

in whispers of a dream of bodies moving.
The credo is never allow anything I don't believe.
I've always sought something I didn't know.

Every obsession finds its place. There's no
tradition to hold on to – nothing but the dance
making visible the promise of a flawless truth.

– after Pina, Wim Wenders, dir. (2011)
and "Lillies of the Valley" (Jun Miyake, composer)

On *The Dark Side of the Moon* or: Around and Through Beyond

There's someone in my head, but it's not me
– "Brain Damage"

Music dates us. Yes. That's something we can't escape. There is a music – a part of its time – that's in us all. Like the famous paradox: does life imitate art, or is it the opposite? – music does define us, but the belief that "we define the music" carries its own truth as well. That truth has its own season. We live our lives anchored in a time, and that time sings its own songs, plays its music, dances its dance. Pink Floyd's *The Dark Side of the Moon* is of my world, my time, my breathing – and I do listen. I don't stop.

Some bursts of light are so extraordinary they blind us for a while. We can't see it all. This is equally true for the music that fills us. There's more each time we take it all in. If Heraclitus had lived in London, March of '73, he would have said – with his headphones on, no doubt – "You can't listen to the same *Dark Side* twice." Every time, the first time. Something new. Some swirling note from a synth, some bend of the string, some voice underneath. And isn't that at least part of the greatness of any recording?

Although I'd heard a few bits of Pink Floyd's early work, nothing prepared me for listening to *Dark Side* the first time, through headphones. Surrounding and immediate. Everything closed off but the music. An incredible moment. David Gilmour wishes he could have heard / experienced *Dark Side* first through headphones: "That would have been something." An impossibility though. Hearing it *first* isn't the same as creating it – from nothing to everything.

This was my first full taste of their music.

The lyrics by Roger Waters? ... Simple; complex. Easy to know; impossible to define. Clichéd; alive. This clashing, a vital part of the greatness. I don't know if the music changed me, but I do know this recording opened my head completely. And I listened more.

In the layers of music, something began to emerge. A shadow moving? Someone lost maybe? Something missing? I listened deep, trying to understand, determine, know – and this continued for years. Then, *boom*. It was Syd Barret. His eyes lurking in the dark, burning toward some fracture, some greedy maw, toward some peace, some silence. The band's former front man, guitarist, vocalist, writer. Now I hear him in all the music, and not just the *Dark Side* sessions.

A relentless specter, Barret ghosts their landscape while the Floyd tries for years & songs & separate lives to carve a world around him/through him/beyond him – but they can't do it. Song after song, the recordings, the tours – he remains:

> "You lock the door and throw away the key"
> – "Brain Damage," *The Dark Side of the Moon*

> "Come on you painter, you piper, you prisoner, and shine"
> – "Shine on You Crazy Diamond," *Wish You Were Here*

> "So have a good drown, as you go down all alone
> Dragged down by the stone"
> – "Dogs," *Animals*

> "I've got wild staring eyes and I've got a strong urge to fly"
> – "Nobody Home," *The Wall*

> "And in my dreams I meet the ghosts"
> – "High Hopes," *The Division Bell*

So Pink Floyd embraced that loss – their loss. But for me it's not just Syd. He's not *the* loss to me. It's something more. Maybe a symbol for something gone in me, something missing, and that's why I hold the music like a thread to follow … why others find connection … and keep finding. 972 weeks on the billboard charts. 45 million units sold – so far. Phenomenal.

From the heartbeat – actually, Nick Mason on kick – which opens the recording and returns at the end, after "Eclipse," and all points in between, the music is such a flip book of imagery, such a phantasmagoria of dream, life and death in a melody – I can't just hear it. I must be the music.

"Dig that hole, forget the sun"

The song "Breathe" comes to me like Dōgen Zenji's words, "One must be deeply aware of the impermanence of the world." All things slipping away. Gilmour sings, "And all you touch, and all you see is all your life will ever be." Nothing lasts. This is true. And we all race like fugitives toward the grave. And this is the opening. Your life is what you make, and then it's gone. I hear this even when it's not playing. A constant truth.

"And I'm not frightened of dying
Any time will do, I don't mind"

Late into the night – dim lights from my player system the only glow – "The Great Gig in the Sky" unfolds its wonder. Clare Tory's voice, primal and beautiful, as magnificent as any instrument could be, fits perfectly when Richard Wright's piano gives way to organ, and the song builds. Her presence on the track somehow becomes a great pivot for the entire album. Tory, who sings without singing, lets me know full well how much can be said without saying anything. The unsaid. There's no real way to describe it; it must be heard.

I remember thinking: *we are afraid*. That hasn't changed, at least not for me.

I want this voice in my body, this howling, so I can close my eyes against the unnamable empty – and know it.

I define myself by those things I hold close – things both sacred and impossible to live without. All the *must haves* I would save from the dreaded fires... My love, my children, my Dad's books, my Mother's voice, two photographs, the words of Bishop, Gilbert, Stafford – *Kind of Blue*, Bergman's *Persona*, my walking stick ... This song is one of them.

"only ordinary"

And here's the contradiction – I don't know myself anymore, or maybe it's the ground I walk that I don't know. Television and news apps that yell. The endless threat. The faces. Words on a page. Bird on the sill. It's all "which is which and who is who". All moments, ordinary in their making – moments that connect the routine days folded into years, and the motion that defines, then suddenly – though it's never sudden – puts on its suit of aching, and the pains blur to hush.

"The time is gone, the song is over
Thought I'd something more to say"

***

1. My life was nothing but edges then. Everything I did. Edges everywhere. I was an immortal – so it seemed.
2. I was never *all*.
3. The world inside my head was a nesting gift – and I'm certain it was the keyboard.
4. Desperation became mantra to whisper into the wind.
5. Like the man in overalls – he never wore a shirt in winter – on the bench outside the college library – the body of a guitar resting on his thigh, its neck pointing deep into clouds – me asking if I could play – his eyes burning through my skull. That was a no.
6. A hole is a hole is a hole – my description. Music as Möbius. If melody were rectangle, if words were thread.
7. There's no one to explain the why. Mad is mad.
8. I listen for the word *choose* – then remember I'm no believer.
9. Nothing like it, before or since. I'm stealing Bradbury now – and turtles, surely, all the way down: When I die, *The Dark Side* is dead.

A September Nevermind

The weak blood of this crescent scoops
a hole into the West, a wound, an opening,
call it a curve where time leaks away – and
the road – and my son riding home from work
tapping music against his knee: "the man
who sold the world": my hard hands to
the hard wheel, conscious of the four and
eight, then turning left, and down the slow
hill, we leave the ghost of Kurt Cobain in my
rearview, a thin groaning in the cross of Weaver
Pike & Rogers Drive, the dash light a bit less
than needed but perfect, somehow pitiless,
like a deep burn, somehow holy, like all those
words that should come but never do

Greatness Was Never Enough ...

"Dark Was the Night, Cold Was the Ground"
– Blind Willie Johnson, 1927,
recording included on Murmurs
of the Earth, *Voyager I disc, 1977*

The cracked soil of southeast Texas
bakes under savanna in swelter until

there's no escaping – no wind or rain
to let the soul breathe while the world

sleeps without knowing all its goodness,
no stories ever giving up their truths

held deep in the fist – no place to be
after fire and rubble steal all things home –

living among the ruins until his lungs
give out – an old man at 48 – nothing left

but silence and a history designed for him
not to fit – decades later, his pocketknife,

a liquid quiver over steel strings, does
find its own way into a long unknown

Not Making Heads or Tails

A Winter Diary ... 1/2018

I broke your heart with the back of my mind
– from a song by John Hiatt

The wipers are frozen to the windshield. I chip & chip. Nothing. Ice, still falling. Mid-twenties today. Exhaust rises as I let the truck warm up. That should do it.

Inside, the fire is enough. My empty cup on the hearth begs a bit more, but two is plenty. Down the hall, I hear The Chromatics on tv: "Someone is stealing you at night." Must be the Roadhouse. Something about shadows and last time and driving.

From the window, a few mourning doves, refuse to let go their spot, huddle on the weeping cherry's bone branches.

The world we think we know isn't the world after all. Sometimes silence is a gift. Sometimes it's the only say we have. But there is the implied, the unsaid. I dreamed a séance class in Honors Hall. The teacher wanted a smoke, and said, "Walk with me." And I did. We crossed the quad. In the dream I loved his long coat.

Ghosts drift the room as if a reckoning were underway, and I'm fine with that. "It has to be." I'd eat *those* words if I could – their tale & plot & landscape or hurt – grind them down with my back teeth, then swallow to keep them hidden, but they'd only sprout in my belly.

The cab must surely be warm by now. Weather channel says the skies should clear by tomorrow. Doesn't matter. This road goes nowhere.

When Bird Plays –

all the music that's ever been
all rage & fire, as if this were
the rhythm of all the bodies,
spins in time with the planet.

Think when there's nothing,
when the only gift, if you listen
close enough, is a burst of colors
in folds of blue or white or red –

to silence. Then storm. Then silence
again. When the eyes look away,
when the hands stop reaching,
there will be this music between us.

Take the petals, sprinkle
them over a drift of snow and forget –
no northbound trains or alleys,
nothing fractured, no more connections,

needles slipping under the skin,
the bloom of a red orchid.
When the fire is in the mouth,
in fingertips, in flesh & smoke

& the noise of God explodes
in every direction – escape,
dissolve, vamoose – like Sisyphus
with a horn blowing the world

along the street's brittle edges
and back, like hidden clusters
of stars wound tight in the hand,
a night in Tunisia – he dies on the couch.

A white man juggles boxes
on television. The crowd roars.
An incessant rain washes down
the loose brick of our darker moods.

– after jazz saxophonist Charlie Parker and his signature
piece, Dizzy Gillespie's "A Night in Tunisia"

"Are You in the Mood?"

The Buddha, after his day
in the winter fields, puts
the disc on the turntable,
lowers the arm

The needle touches vinyl
with a pop,
then a sweet hiss –

Django Reinhardt, May 1936 –
How the dead go on living

And me, at my computer screen,
fingers tapping keys
well after midnight
while the heater's fan hums
against the cold

II

Duets:

Silent Stars and Hushed Rivers

**A Love Poem for Past & Future
Squeezed Tightly into Now**

*a treasure for the poor to find
– Townes Van Zandt, "If I Needed You"*

Winter is here with its bitter, prophetic rage.
The cattle, huddled under trees, know what to do.
Smoke rises along the road to the lake.
At the bottom of the well, cool water over dark.
And the years blur past us, a streak of frames
in motion telling yet another story.

I've heard your voice

    If I needed you

showing the muscle in my chest the way – your eyes
a window, your hands a truth as you talk me
through the night.

Birds are stirring. Sunrise over the ridge colors the wind:
the field an easel, the fence a brush, your words are
mountains, a tremble of leaves over the ground

    Would you come to me

in the whatever of the whenever – *if* is a lonely place.

I know pain waits for me, and silence will open
its beautiful head. Before the room empties,
before the bits of talk fall to the floor then
disappear, before these walls echo dreams
under rocks in the river east of here, you can
tell me – you can tell me one more time
the hole inside of everything – your breath
on my cheek to keep my eyes from closing.

You'll touch my hand

    I would swim the sea

and the stars at midnight will be my only map.

Grievous Angel

He lifts a smoky chin over sand
& cactus & lizard, settles in
against the stars above Joshua Tree,

against the beat of legend,
the click of train to rail until
his gray puffs of bone
come to nothing

            The words say
wild horses run the flatland to where
the only music is wind over rock –

a mirage of silent curves & sin
(his own) with mounds of bottles,
with pools of goodness

            – after the documentary Gram Parsons:
            Fallen Angel *(2004), Gandulf Hennig, dir.*

Gravel Roads

Nothing's where I left it before
Set of keys and a dusty suitcase
– Lucinda Williams

Her words carry all the ache and groove
of a southern road in deep fall when empty
trees have their stories to tongue in the wind –
in the creakings that justify all missing parts

while the river moans its slow darkness –
Can you hear it? – toward the colors of dawn
that will leave the sky while we're watching
though we'll never see the moment when

If you ever catch the words mid-air – hold them
cupped in both hands – like lightning bugs
with their yellows pouring from the cracks
between your fingers – and then – release

Some Say He Was Never There at All

– a cento

"I'll tell you all my secrets since
the face forgives the mirrors.
Everyone's looking for someone

to blame. There's a place on my arm
where I've written: *Tear the promise
from my heart*. With a steeple full of

swallows, I want to believe in the mercy
of the world again. Never leave a trace or
forget another yellow moon has punched

a hole – There's no light in the tunnel,
no irons in the fire. I dreamed someday
I'd go, and the road was like a ribbon –

but you're innocent when you dream.
I disappear in your name."

– Tom Waits
December 1978, Austin, Texas

A Beast with his Horn

With no idea how I got here – but thanks to
L Cohen – I can hear the rattle in my throat

and know the time is closer than when my days
were handed to me by period and *get up now* –

or the easy ache of summer – and what have I done
in the meantime? "Nothing," you say. "You're right,"

I say, then let both lips touch, knowing my mask is
on the table where I left it, my soul in a jar by the bed.

There must be a bird somewhere – somewhere a line
that follows the morning to its stillness, to its heat,

its turn to yawning and beautiful darks that never let go.
There is more than one. There must be a hole somewhere,

and a shoulder digging for the sake of digging only –

– after Leonard Cohen's "Famous Blue Raincoat"

Urge for Going

– after the song by Joni Mitchell

The last of summer geese,
such a thin silhouette of grace,
ride an ache of cold much older

than rocks. They haunt the sky's
steel gray to empty blue over fields
no human eye will see turn to brown,

no boot will trail through restless snows,
no ear for wind among the bristle cones.
When night comes, let the silent stars

and hushed rivers keep their dreams –
When night comes, let the fields pray
the only way they can: the letting go.

"I don't know, I don't know"

Little girl, living in the hard shadows
of mountains, crossing railroad tracks
to play Bach, crows in the deep woods,
fingers on the keys for hours every day –
what do you fear?

Did someone tell you your dreams
should stay small? tell you the world
would punish you for being you?
How do you wrestle – blow by blow –
all your demons to the ground?

Tell me the rage, the ache of work,
the passion in your eyes and mouth –
how to scream with no sound,
no voice, no words.

To be beaten – and to beat – is
this the life we make?
Teach me how to play a song like
no one else has ever played.

> *Gonna break this chain off and run*
> *I'm gonna lay down somewhere shady*
> *– Nina Simone*

21ˢᵗ Century Schizoid Sonnet

– King Crimson as soundtrack

The rich tableaux –
leaf to forest to wind
in the middle of
concrete and steel
where splintered
promises and broken
chains for puppet jaws
freeze the tongues
above the news crawler
then give way to mantra:
forget the napalm
bring the iPhone
The wars are
in the street

The Weight

– West Saugerties, New York, 1968,
a conversation,
Luis Buñuel and Robbie Robertson

Guilt and loss ride your back with its dark humps
into streets with no names or numbers for direction,
and you've no idea where to go or even why both feet
are moving, scuffing over sidewalk – the soundtrack
for your small regrets, the doings and undoings –
but you walk on.

Window by window, door by door, through caravans
of color and flowers and smoke. Faces smudge by
for you to forget and be forgotten.

Lost books or moon or bridges.

The will to change, the need to say whatever comes
to mind, to make something where there's nothing.

Take this stone from your troubled eye, lift it to my
hard shoulder – my breathing, a map for your hands –
then let me walk.

Follow my shadows into all uncertainty as if one tiny

act of voice, a wisp of long-time-coming, could change
anything. Lift your mouth and bruise the air:
Forgiveness is a terrible word in any language.

No Endings, No Beginnings

I just decided I wanted to become someone else...
So I became someone else.
— Dusty Springfield

The dust of stars follows me
into the silence as if what was
thought or hoped the moon
could do — light dripping its arc
to dawn, my words breathed
across uncertainties — making
my burn of youth, all those years
stacked upon each other, lose
the road *here* — and looking back?

— as if wanting were enough — only
a reminder, an almost something
that can't quite come to focus —
letting go the child maybe or rain
in the trees, a hillside graveyard,
with its names of promise, smells
of roast in the oven, Saturdays
in town, or my radio under the pillow
"like a circle in a spiral," that summer

of finding but no way to hold on —

the mirror with its fever of *can do
anything*, of the need that was my life –
I remember scribbled words that dog me
now – keeping them in a puzzle box,
letting no one see, wanting and not
wanting – words I could slip into –
afraid to jump, afraid to speak a truth
to life – with its dark threads of DNA

Stories in "Flamenco Sketches"

– after the song by Miles Davis

*The sound, muted and open, is not unlike that of a
flamenco singer – intense, introspective, defiant, lonely,
and at times delicately passionate. – Nat Hentoff*

One candle by the bed gives enough light. Our skin
grows young in it.

There's no hurry in these hands, no hurry in the scale
of bass & piano. The drum has the rub of our bodies
in its brush.

The trumpet has no quiver in its heat. It backs down
to where we hold each other.

This is my story:
We talk the hours into anger, into sadness, into prophecy.
We say all the words until nothing is left but sleep. I lay
a finger against your left temple to feel the music. I watch
you breathe, and that moving is like no other. Somewhere
in all this I learn that life is whole, without stitch or seam
or beginning. We listen to the wind and we know the wind
and the voice are everything.

*

It snows most of the night, four inches by daybreak,
then the saxophone takes over.

    *

This is your story:
There's a certain pain in beauty, a certain rage in the body
like blue fire, like the rhythm of space, all things spreading
out from the center, like a pale flower, like a woman or
a man, like the place of songs, like the feel of darkness.

    *

You blow out the candle. Strings of smoke stretch
to the ceiling before they turn invisible and leave us.

This is the song:
   "Flamenco Sketches"
delicate
delicate
a low heat

on fire

in fire
of fire

always fire
always

    for Mary

Notes for an Essay on Points of Crossing

*I will be happy if the English reader sees
behind descriptions of the life...*
– Mikhail Sholokhov, forward to Quiet Flows the Don

"Where have all the graveyards gone? Long time ago" – That's Pete Seeger. He's singing at my writing table into the soft darkness of my room – my comfort – my changing with every letter that clicks to the page. It's the power of song. And I wish I had it – with my own writing, I mean.

I wanted some music to let me know just how short it all is. Something to let me know how impossible my words are. But it's a trick I won't master. Something to say, but no way to get at it. I can write what it's about – I can't write the thing itself.

So I write these words: *heart, chair, candle, phone.* It's all math. There's nothing real. Just symbols, figures, marks against the stillness. Are they signs? Maybe. Something to learn? Who can say –

I do like flowers though. I do. My favorite? Hibiscus. It changes color from morning to afternoon – or at least the hybrid I have does. So short. A striking breath of lovely, then it's gone.

What we say and do matters – or that's what I would like to believe, to know. The truth is – it's an empty well. A dark abiding. But I'm ok with that. Every loss lets me know there's more where that came from. There's nothing I could ever do to change that. And this "nothing" looks and acts like something.

A spin to darkness. The terrible waiting. The pointless smooth stone rolling down the pointless worn hill. Here I am again – picking it up. Where have all the flowers gone? They never left. They're still here.

III

Streaming:

Coming Unhinged – Unhinged Already

Be Here to Love Me

My life will run out before my work does.
I've designed it that way. – Townes Van Zandt

Broken down van by the railroad tracks behind
the liquor store, barrel fires & coffee grounds –
The highway from Galveston to Lubbock,
from Clarksville to Fort Worth – irrational, wild.

Something for the writing – motel room after
room after room – the curtains drawn, no way
to *believe* the day from night. Lost pages
never found.
                A childhood is missing. All parts

telling who & what & how & why – gone,
burned away –
                Dust swept to the corners, then
left alone.
                Only the music holds him here –
like a rope or chain or ribbon
of breath –
                the deepest silence of grey on grey,
then a splatter of stars against the moonless sky.

   – *after* Be Here to Love Me, *a film by Margaret Brow*

Storm

"Cumbia and Jazz Fusion," recording by
Charles Mingus, NYC, 10 March 1977

Birds throat the jungle to life –
squawking green to percussion
to oboe, bassoon.
That's how the song begins –
but what I can't see when I listen
is Mingus's shoulders, wood curving
from his belly, both hands
on the upright's long neck –
and no way to know
that in his hands, in the music,
in darkness between recording

and this room, years away,
where I sit listening,
amyotrophic lateral sclerosis,
an impatient ghost,
is beginning its own
flexed pleasure paradigm
in the pulled bars of the bass clef
at song's end – in the fade.

I lift my own right hand –

so recently under the surgeon's knife,
the wrist letting go its lump
– and trill my fingers, for circulation,
in counter to the coup d'état
of trumpet and sax whose blare
is a red sun bearing down
on the warm sea – a last border
where colors blend
to deep and perfect silence.

And then I sleep – my head filling
with thick, wet trees
and river gods and boats run aground.

In the morning – you remove
the bandage, kiss my opened palm,
dress the wound

while January, fresh-pillared
in wood smoke, gives up
its first snow to our roof.

After Listening to "Neptune, the Mystic,"
during a Winter Storm, Jan. 2011

– for Edison Jennings

Water, blue with its Danube ghost of another past,
fills my ears, overflows my arms, this soft chair,
this room. I float – a heavy silence – fingers and hair
drifting the dark shimmers of cold.

The strings sketch a beauty in snow
in the voice that trails the hall with her perfect hush
of the bent word, the voice that gives up its sharpest edge
to waiting. I've no way of saying what's to be said,

so I offer nothing. A hollow moment.
Clear enough. What the young will believes
and what the well-spent life only supposes
never meet in real time. The hours turn
upon themselves, taking the sack of grieving,
stuffed and angry, to both thin shoulders.

– Neptune, the Mystic, the 7ᵗʰ movement of The Planets,
Op. 32, an orchestral suite by Gustav Holst, 1914-1916

Enharmonics

depth, delicacy, and display
– Glenn Gould, 1955

All extremities of a will to do
and be find their own way among
the fragments of glove and chair
and dread.

                There's a perfect edge
to knowing.

                Such a delicate tapping
of fingers, such transcendent abandon
to song.

                The fragile thread of self
to other holds seam as long as it can –
and then the tearing free – so much
to mean beyond the words.

                A coat,
a scarf worn just so in the wind's last
measure of solitude, an Aria played
as if the mind were a slow curve of sky
to nothing.

                The trees and water go on,
while the melody stills to silence.

    *

Everything a performance. No repetition, no connection
outside. Everything an otherness. Outside a repetition of
water land and sky. Everything a stone with nothing left.

Nothing ever before could sound like this, could be this, so
why do that? Find another moment, another fire to connect
with. Everything a performance. And while he's playing,

I'll let you know what my mind is since just now my mind
is – Variation 25 – his with no space between whatsoever,
no separation because of time, tape & speaker, or things as

arbitrary as life and death *immortal unspeakable inimitable*
but now no more tape. A digital file, then point and click.
I'm writing words on a page I could not to save my life have

anticipated – some wandering herd crossing a plain and
for the first time seeing a mountain but having no way to
process it. It just is. Leave it at that. Let the music rest. Lift

your fingers from the keys, and rest. A moment, a sprinkle
of shade, a path no one walks. Now walk that. The music is
the delicate seam of beauty, the rare unspeakable truth that

will not be resisted, and I never do. Another reminder of
the frailty, of the chance I had mistaken for my life or what
others so close to the music might have thought they knew.

So go ahead, so go ahead feel the notes, feel the melody
that swallows you whole. There was silence – but only for
a moment, then the force of God maybe, I couldn't say,

moved the troubled waters while I played. Who will sing
now? In the recordings I play on – into all the dark years
and more – note after flawless note – to find sense where

there is none. No way to explain what the music means or
how I drift on melody – a blot & staff between lines in
the treble clef, slipping to stillness with something to say

but no itch to speak, so I sing, and cannot stop. The body's
threads of nerve and loss find their perfection in possibility
– in the apostrophed silences I never want to end.

    *

Tell me again how much you will miss
the music – with its halls and windows,
its doors and cabinets.

                    Morning drifts
the lake – a mist to rub the eaves with
greatness.

                  Tell me what will
become of the world you have made.

                  And tell me
the cost, if you can, if you remember –

Tell me if you feel it in the swaying of
your head toward the final notes,

                lifting
both hands like beautiful wings – dropping
your head. A long prayer to black silence.

Aria da capo, 1981

Amsterdam

...postcard:

Ssshhh – Don't tell anyone. I'm outside the hotel room
where Chet Baker died. What made him think he could fly?
I bribed the bellboy to let me in to see the window.
My fingers against the cool glass – the city, a cluster
of lights waiting for dawn, and suddenly I feel wings –
I swear – opening from both my shoulders.
See you soon. Maybe –

1994

Mirrors

I'll be your mirror
Reflect what you are, in case you don't know
I'll be the wind, the rain and the sunset
The light on your door to show that you're home
– The Velvet Underground & Nico, 1967

1. *I Was Told What It Means*

L'Olympia, Paris, October 1969

To be a dragon with fire, a tongue for
every soul, a body for your darkness
you cannot resist – That's what I am,
all rough-edged and new – I'll break
your heart, and there's nothing you
will do to stop it – I'm the monster
in your ear, the shaking in your brain,
the hammer that cracks open your world –
And the slivers fly a lifetime from here

2. *Give Me Your Hands*

Trident, London, 1972

The life electric in the street
beside K West keeps all its glitter
and flesh intact for a world of
pastels and feathers – "like a
slow voice on a wave of phase,"
Ziggy sang – while the stars,
anchored to their darkness,
tremble and moan with
the music's dip and surge

3. Same as It Ever Was

Talking Heads, Compass Point,
New Providence, July 1980

Unless we cook the moment –
unless the melody attacks itself
and words eat the stories they tell
– knowing we've never arrived is
how it must begin – so how can we
know when we get *here* – or *there* –
if you can tell any difference at all –
wherever *they* may be, but that's not
as real as how are we going to stay

4. *Body of Sorrow*

Berlin, 1987

In the ruined bar of the Hotel
Esplanade, Potsdamer Platz,
with its angels, its trapeze artists –
this must be how the living
ghost the dead – Nick Cave finds
forever in his voice scratching
against the bodies in the room
and the lives they do not live,
in the silence hidden at the core

5. *Voices*

> *Tie yourself to me*
> *– P.J. Harvey, September 1993*

The haunts of crossing a desert
of city-time and small talk – all
that necessary obliging for the
expected life – are never prepared
for the slicked-back grit and certainty
of a woman whose time has come,
whose voice is found, whose world
she makes alone, whose only need
is the next word she tongues

6. *Please*

     St. Vincent, 2017

From martyrs in leather to
exotic colors of the mouth –
her words are otherworldly,
a guide for the bump & grind
under storms of light to burn
the brain while the fuzz tightens
its rage – and the bend of fingers
on steel strike the hypno closing
for all the stories in our blood

7. *Every Restless Night*

Sinéad O'Connor, 1992/2023

Yell at me, shout me down,
I'll keep singing though it rips
my soul, though it slaps me hard.
I can stand. I grew my hair long,
but I couldn't find me, so I shaved
it off. They killed me. They buried
my body, but I'm a seed. Listen for
me – in the rain along the streets and
in the fields. I'll rise on the wind.

Unassuming Almost Sonnet, Spring 2020

– listening to Roebuck Staples

The asparagus fern on the porch post
explains what the wind is saying
There is never one Ozymandias
There are shadows And I should
know it by now Shadows that
never leave the path They rise
Miserable fists pumping the air
They follow They point They poke
murmur murmur murmur They
blot out the way home and I'm
lost again But *I've made up my
mind* keeps telling me walk walk
walk There is a bed There's a roof
in the cold rain There is a table
and words to keep me full

A Tao of Country Music

– a cento,

T for thanks, thanks a lot. T for too much,
for throwing horseshoes over my left shoulder,
for three white horses (not six) – and all blinded
fools who hit the big time. T for the race is on,
for a tiger by the tail, for too blue to fly.

If I only have one eye to see with, I only cry half as
much. Hear the rumble? It's Sin City. Kern River. Crazy.
I've come in search of Jesus or Owen Bradley – six days
on the road with thick smoke, dim lights, and prison.
Another day older, a man of means, a ring of fire.

The t - r - o - u - b - l - e with you don't have to call me
darlin' is that you won't believe, can't believe, the things
a heart will tell the mind, unless you're strong enough
to bend that is, but it's all right, 'cause it's midnight, and
we've got four walls, four strong winds for the good times.

Tell my why, Wanda Jackson – before the next teardrop
falls – if you could live life over, would you? Rabon dies
of lung cancer, then Alton moves to Huntsville, sells
door-to-door. Ira smashes all his mandolins just so
Charlie can sing with Melba. Hank buys a hamburger,

his last – but the road goes on forever. Diamonds and dirt.
No sadness, no sorrow from Austin City to Bakersfield to
16th Avenue, The Bluebird, Jack Clement's Cowboy Arms
Hotel & Recording Spa. God bless the boys & girls. God
bless the boys & girls and their pens that drip sacred ink.

Hey! Townes Van Zandt! Some good words for you: rain
& playthings & snake eyes. Don't feel bad or be disappointed
on the corner of love & heartache. Liars one, believers zero.
We don't live there anymore. It's a sea of heartbreak – It's
where fools collide. So pop a top and turn your radio on –

Listen. Hear it? The last train from Poor Valley. Sometimes
you're on a lost highway. Sometimes you're a desperado
waiting in lonesome standard time. All the stars are fallen.
The silence of purple skies over Lake Pontchartrain sings
in tongues of silver, sings in lullabies and legends –

until the cows come home.

for David James

Horses

– CBGB, East Village,
Winter 1975

When that music's hot subway steel & backroom smoke
hits your spine, you can't help but follow, can you? She's
the NY hard-mouthed poet punk of the street, all sidewalk
grit & barfly. Goat woman from (not in) an Aquarian age –
a neuter gendered prophet of the microphone – with a spew
of blood from her raw-edged siren throat to boil through
every vein. In the land of a thousand dances & spoons, her
tongue's a rage against any light, a Molotov cocktail to
your deepest ear. The heavy skyline crumbles in on itself,
night after month after year, to an orgy of poster-plastered
brick & sweat – always on the down beat. *Jesus died for
somebody's sins, but not mine*, she says, and the studio
apartment parties tilt their way across the floor
in a forest of legs, in a bowl of hands.

– after the album Horses *by Patti Smith*

1968 A Floating Sky, Shimmering

The world was coming unhinged – unhinged already – but we didn't know it, couldn't see it then, too busy with head trips & madness & blood in our dreams.

Something was hiding, and to name it would have missed the point – *I look at the floor, and I see it needs sweeping.*

When the *White Album* hit the streets, we took it with us everywhere, for days, ready to play at a moment's notice, to study, to listen with a nod – less is more – as though it were sacred text, the lines telling us how to live – so we lived.

We spun the lps backward for tales of the dead, unrelenting in our pursuit of some pop frenzy we could never quite touch – the sort of thing that disappears the closer you move to it, but we never stopped trying.

This was the end.

Another life would have understood, would have found something to hold on to – like a drawing I remember from my father's study wall – a rider and horse, both heads down – the slow thump of hooves against a stony path, the sun easing deeper into mesa.

Taking Notes

When the lights shut off
And it's my turn to settle down
My main concern
Promise that you will sing about me
— Kendrick Lamar, "Sing About Me, I'm Dying of Thirst"

Promise that you will write about me
Promise that you will write about me
Promise me – promise me
Promise my words you won't forget my hand –
      writing its story – my hand wrapped
      against the pain I didn't even know was there –
      deep in the tendons and bone – Promise
      my voice that screams when no one's there,
      no one to listen, no one to witness, no one
      to give me their tears – I'm thirsty

Promise, promise that you will – Won't you? –
      wrapped against the wound of too much
      empty page and not enough story to leave
      behind, and *that* is my aggravation – Pity
      that it's not more real, not more human, not
      more necessary – If I didn't say another word –
      no dreams would be lost – Nobody changes
      who they are – I'm a blip on the blip of a blip –

That's all – Nothing more – That's *my* aggravation –
too nothing for the something –
Promise me – I am thirsty

Promise me – Please – that you won't forget the old with
　　the new – I'll be gone, yes, so promise you'll write
　　about me, that you will bring the words that aren't
　　yet tired – bring words that can say something new –
　　Promise me my obituary telling won't be the end of it
　　– I'm tired of breathing, don't you know – If I only
　　had a cup of water, then my thirst would go away,
　　would disappear – just like my eyes, my voice, my
　　hand – Promise that – Promise that you – Promise
　　that you will remember all the unfortunate hurt and
　　dream – that you'll write about me even if words are
　　nothing since even nothing is something – What's
　　not said – What's not written – Even
　　the empty has its shape

Promise that you will say – when you write – all the truth
　　I never could – Promise me – Promise a mellow jazz
　　in the air to the empty chairs, to the empty hallway
　　where no one walks – Let the jazz play – Let John
　　Coltrane squeeze his unexplainable into my ear –
　　when you read the words to give me shape – words
　　that Frankenstein all my notions that are long gone –
　　the kind of gone which can never be filled no matter

how much is said because the words are always
about, they never *are* – they're about the thing and
not the thing – but promise me any way – I'm thirsty
– I'm tired – No more running – No more
pop, pop, pop on the keys

Promise that you will – no matter what, no matter where,
        no matter how big the dark space between *here* and
        then – Promise me – That's all I'm asking –
        a promise for a lost cause, my lost cause – Me –
        I am the *cause* – I am the *lost* – There's no saving
        the silence – no way to find when it's too far gone –
        And it is

Promise that you'll dream about me – that you'll say
        to the future, the one which can never be –
        He was – Promise me – your pinkie, your heart,
        your Mother in the grave – Promise me you'll
        dream and write it down – then burn it
        at midnight – Any midnight will do – If
        you don't write it, it didn't happen –
        If you don't, write, I wasn't there – So
        write it, then – Promise me

Promise you will write down this wrong – Write it,
        Elizabeth said – my wrong – my bad – my one
        sad eye which never closes – never unsees –

Promise you'll leave all the answers – even
the ones you don't have and never did –
Promise me – I'm thirsty – I don't care what
you did or did not – don't care what you
thought or should not – There's no time
like a future past to save your soul –
It's real if you feel it – if you speak it

Promise that you will – There's no time – that
  you will write about me, then
  turn off the lights,
  let the darkness finish,
  let the music play on – play on – play on –

Chicago, the Earl of Old Town

...postcard:

Sometimes the words don't come. They hide –
too true too caring too unwilling – as if to say
by not saying. There are holes with no bottom,
skies that are nothing but cloud. Sometimes

the hard truth is a wrinkle in my stomach, an ache
where nothing is, a stare through the closed window.
We can whisper: he is gone, she is gone – but
that never tells the whole story, does it?

Maybe we *can* do without doing. Maybe so.
Or at least know the stars are listening.

– John Prine, with Hello – if you say it
1971

...a reply:

From my table, the morning
in hand with coffee steam –
almost as if I willed it,
the pileated woodpecker,
large and mystical, floats
to the cherry's trunk,
an effortless beauty,
a special moment of good
on such dark days, then goes.

– S
April 2020

When the music's over
Turn out the lights
– The Doors

Notes and Sources

"A World Full of Lies": *No Direction Home* (2005), Martin Scorsese, dir.; "Lay Down Your Weary Tune," the title of a song by Dylan

"Quartet in C Minor, Op. 18, No. 4": a fictionalized modern setting and an equally fictional review; in section one, Homer's Odysseus (O.) and Penelope (P.); lyrics at the end of each section from "Tales of Brave Ulysses," a song by Cream; musical notations for each section, The Guarneri Quartet's 1970 recording of Quartet in C Minor, Op. 18, No. 4 – *Beethoven, The Six Early Quartets, Opus 18*, RCA

"Exile on Main St.": Nellcôte, the villa in France where the Stones recorded the tracks for *Exile on Main St.*

"A September Nevermind": *Nevermind*, studio album by Nirvana; "The Man Who Sold the World," a David Bowie song performed live by Nirvana

"Not Making Heads or Tales": John Hiatt's "Tip of My Tongue" and "Saturday" by The Chromatics

"Are You in the Mood?": a song written by Django Reinhardt and Stéphane Grappelli, recorded by Quintette du Hot Club de France in 1936

Duets: The symbol ∞ separates the poems into pairs.

"Grievous Angel": In 1973, Gram Parsons died of an overdose in a motel room near Joshua Tree, California. He'd made an agreement with his friend Phil Kaufman – when one of them died, the other would cremate the body at Joshua Tree National Park, spreading the ashes there. Kaufman and a friend stole Parsons's body from the L.A. International Airport and fulfilled the singer's wishes. Parsons, with Emmylou Harris, recorded *Grievous Angel*, his final studio album, earlier that same year.

"I don't know, I don't know": *What Happened, Miss Simone?* (2015), documentary, Liz Garbus, dir.

"The Weight": The conversation between Robbie Robertson, The Band's songwriter and guitarist, and Luis Buñuel, filmmaker, is fictitious, although Buñuel's films did influence Robertson as he was writing "The Weight".

"No Endings, No Beginnings": Dusty Springfield's cover of "The Windmills of Your Mind"

"Storm": Charles Mingus, during the 1977 "Cumbia" recording sessions, was experiencing undiagnosed, early stages of amyotrophic lateral sclerosis (ALS).

"After Listening to 'Neptune, the Mystic,' during a Winter Storm, Jan. 2011": The occasion for this poem was the tragic death of a close friend's daughter.

"Enharmonics": Glenn Gould's recordings (1955, 1981) of Bach's *The Goldberg Variations* and the 2009 film *Genius Within: The Inner Life of Glenn Gould*, Michèle Hozer and Peter Raymont, dirs.

"Amsterdam": Chet Baker, the jazz trumpeter and vocalist, fell to his death from a hotel window or balcony in Amsterdam, 1988. The cause of Baker's fall, shrouded in mystery, is undetermined. His death was ruled accidental.

"Mirrors": The Velvet Underground & Nico; the once lost recording of Led Zeppelin's concert in Paris (October 1969), rediscovered in 2007; David Bowie's recording *The Rise and Fall of Ziggy Stardust and the Spiders from Mars*; the *Remain in Light* sessions by Talking Heads; Nick Cave's work with Wim Wenders on the film *Der Himmel über Berlin*; P. J. Harvey's live performance on *The Tonight Show*; St. Vincent's live appearance on *Austin City Limits*; Sinéad O'Connor's jeered performance at the Bob Dylan Tribute Concert in 1992 and her death in 2023

"1968 A Floating Sky, Shimmering": the White Album (*The Beatles*, 1968); lps (long playing vinyl records)

"Chicago, the Earl of Old Town": The Earl of Old Town was a music club in Chicago, featuring folk artists. John Prine, a member of Chicago's folk revival, became a victim of the COVID-19 pandemic, dying in April 2020.

Acknowledgements

I'm grateful to Amantine Brodeur and Maureen Seaton for their close readings of the ms. Also, thanks to the editors of the following publications in which these poems, sometimes in earlier versions, first appeared:

52/250, Avatar, Bending Genres, BigCityLit, BOXCAR Poetry Review, Erosha, FRiGG, Iodine Poetry Journal, Istanbul Literary Review, Love in the Time of COVID, Memoir Mixtape, MiPOesias, PoetsArtists, Ramshackle Review, Santa Fe Literary Review, Six Sentences, THIS Literary Magazine, Urban Spaghetti, and *Writer's Quill*

"Be Here to Love Me" was published as a broadside by *MiPOesias.* "Stories in 'Flamenco Sketches'" was nominated by *Erosha* for the Pushcart Prize. "Amsterdam" and "Chicago, the Earl of Old Town" appeared in *A Cluster of Lights: an Anthology,* a collected work from *52/250.* "Not Making Heads or Tales" appeared in *The Bending Genres Anthology 2018/2019.*

Cover art: *Descanso* by Cheryl McPeek Dodds
Author's photo: Mary Rasnake